Goldilocks
and the
Three Bears

First published in 2001 by
Franklin Watts
96 Leonard Street
London
EC2A 4XD

Franklin Watts Australia
45-51 Huntley Street
Alexandria
NSW 2015

A CIP catalogue record for this book is available
from the British Library.

ISBN 0 7496 4049 9 (hbk)
ISBN 0 7496 4225 4 (pbk)

Series Editor: Louise John
Series Advisor: Dr Barrie Wade
Series Designer: Jason Anscomb

Printed in Hong Kong

Goldilocks
and the
Three Bears

by Barrie Wade

Illustrated by Kristina Stephenson

W

FRANKLIN WATTS
LONDON•SYDNEY

Once upon a time there were three bears.

One morning, the three
bears went for a walk,
leaving their porridge
to cool.

A little girl called Goldilocks
was out walking, too.

Goldilocks went inside the three bears' cottage and found their porridge.

Daddy Bear's porridge was much too hot.

Mummy Bear's porridge
was much too cold.

But Baby Bear's porridge
was just right and
Goldilocks ate it all up!

Goldilocks was full so she sat down for a rest.

Daddy Bear's chair was much too hard.

Mummy Bear's chair was much too soft.

Baby Bear's chair was just right ...

... but Goldilocks was too big and the chair broke!

Goldilocks went upstairs
for a sleep.

Daddy Bear's bed was much too hard.

Mummy Bear's bed was
much too soft.

But Baby Bear's bed was just right. Goldilocks lay down and fell fast asleep.

Soon, the three bears
came back from their walk.

"Someone's been eating my porridge," said Daddy Bear.

"Someone's been eating my porridge," said Mummy Bear.

"Someone's been eating my porridge," cried Baby Bear, "and they've eaten it all up!"

"Someone's been sitting in
my chair," said Daddy Bear.

"Someone's been sitting in my chair," said Mummy Bear.

"Someone's been sitting in my chair," cried Baby Bear, "and they've broken it!"

The three bears went
upstairs.

"Someone's been sleeping in my bed," said Daddy Bear.

"Someone's been sleeping in my bed," said Mummy Bear.

"Someone's been sleeping in my bed," cried Baby Bear, "and she's still there!"

Goldilocks woke up, jumped
out of the bed and ran
away as fast as she could.

"Oh, dear," cried Baby
Bear, "I didn't want to
scare her away!"

Leapfrog has been specially designed to fit the requirements of the National Literacy Strategy. It offers real books for beginning readers by top authors and illustrators.

There are 25 Leapfrog stories to choose from: